HORSES & HUMANS

Lucy Sewill

Foreword by Monty Roberts

For Roger who has been beside me on a horse longer than anyone, for my children, Hugo, Ben and Zara, and for Nutty my chestnut friend and my horse of a lifetime.

Peridot Press

First Published 2016 by Peridot Press

12 Deben Mill Business Centre, Old Maltings Approach, Woodbridge, Suffolk IP12 1BL

Tel: 01394 389850 Fax: 01394 386893
Email: enquiries@peridot.co.uk
Website: www.peridot.co.uk

ISBN: 978 1 911382 04 1

Set and designed by Theoria Design (www.theoriadesign.com)

Printed and bound in Great Britain

Foreword

Lucy Sewill brings to her work a list of unique qualities that provides the world with collective talent far greater than which is expected of the family of authors we have been accustomed to. Lucy has lived a lifetime filled with a love for horses that has molded her career. She honored me with a visit to my California farm in August of 2016. It was there that I met Lucy and her husband Roger for the first time. I expected to meet a photographer along with a husband who was accompanying her on the trip. What I actually met were two horse lovers, one of which was an artist with a camera. Some of Lucy's techniques were well off the beaten path when it comes to the photographers I have worked with in the past.

Lucy explained that she much preferred to photograph horses without man-made equipment on them. She stated that she wanted them to be as free as possible to express their inner feelings in reflection of what was happening around them. Coupled with that, she wanted a human connection and the two should intertwine to the extent that there appeared to be a joyous bond between human and horse. Lucy was not concerned about an aesthetic background or colors of any kind. It was her goal to eliminate distracting factors, work in black and white and bring to the pages of her book the collective souls of human and horse. While the method was new for me, it met front and center with the essence of my work.

Some will know that my work has a centerpiece of causing the horse to want to complete a desired task rather than making the horse achieve the goal chosen by the human counterpart. It took me a few hours to realize how close Lucy's concepts were to the very core of what I have attempted to accomplish with the work I call 'Join-Up.' Lucy asked me to put horses in areas and positions not easy to accomplish, but I had a few unique equine characters that helped us meet the requirements. I recall telling Lucy that I could ask Shy Boy to come right into our classroom where we conduct courses at our Monty Roberts International Learning Center here on Flag is Up Farms in Solvang, California.

We continued our work, which included an extensive tour of the farm so that Lucy could get to know each of the areas that might serve well to accomplish her goals. Roger was a very helpful part of the team during the course of the time they spent with me. As the visit was nearing its conclusion, Lucy quietly asked me if I thought it was possible to bring Shy Boy into the saloon that is part of our home. I explained that while he had never been inside the house, it was also true that he had never refused to go anywhere I requested of him. I quipped that he just may want to play a game of pool and the first thing he did was to play with the cue balls by pushing them to and fro with his nose.

The visit of Lucy happened to coincide with an ongoing course that we call Monty's Special Training. They were interested enough to stay as long as possible and actually take part in the course by conducting Join-Ups with horses totally strange to them. It was clear to me that this was a decision made to gain as much information as possible about how horses think and how they respond to their human counterparts. Lucy is not simply a photographer. She is a student of horses and the equine thought processes that create personalities within the behavioral patterns of Equus, the flight animal. This allows Lucy to bring to her book three separate talents that enhance her photography dramatically.

It has come to my attention that, while creating this book, Lucy completed one trip to a distant land where she was to photograph some very beautiful horses. It's true that the subject horses were quite extraordinary and sensitive, but the handling of these horses was unacceptable. They were struck and treated harshly right from the outset of her visit. Lucy announced that she would not accept the conditions provided. The individuals involved were angry and suggested that these actions were necessary to control the horses. Lucy left the facility and the country without bringing home any images of horse or human for her book.

When this information came to me, Lucy and I had already finished our work in California. The actions she took did not surprise me in the least. This is a lady who brings to her pages a love of horses, a desire to create a better world for them and an artistic skill with a camera. This along with an internal understanding of how to read the soul of the individuals in her lens creates within her an individual who each of us should congratulate, enjoy and appreciate. The memory of the visit with Lucy and Roger will stay with me for the rest of my days. Shy Boy will always thank Lucy for allowing him a ticket to the inside of our home, one of the few places he had never visited before Lucy came to Flag is Up.

Monty Roberts
August 2016

Introduction

Horses fill my earliest memories and there is a picture in my mind of all the horses and ponies I have ever known. In fact I have a whole herd of horses past and present in my head.

As a child everything about them was good to me: the smell, the feel, the sense of power they gave and the escape they provided. Whether I was on their backs or on the ground I wanted to be near them and if I wasn't with them I was dreaming about them. I was safe with horses, they protected me and together we were invincible.

As a child there was Solitare, a kind ancient pony who had only one eye and would willingly canter when you just said the word. Merlin, small and fast who took me over my first jump. Caruso who landed me in gorse bushes and Shetland Diana, the cleverest pony I have ever known.

Into adulthood there is Nifty the worried ex-hurdler who was breathtakingly fast but alarmingly couldn't gallop in a straight line. Bob, the huge shire cross who took me hunting. Then there are the Appaloosas

I bred for the spots, the horses I had as foals and the ones I kept until the end of their days. And dear Nutty, my beautiful chestnut friend who shared 19 years of life with me and hundreds of miles of togetherness. These are just a few and there are many more. Some were mine, some I passed on, but all have left their mark on me.

And these were more than just horses to me.

From the start I was a baby too small and early for this world so I was taken from my mother and put in an incubator. They hoped I would live but my mother was told to go home and expect me to die. So we both missed all the initial intimate moments that last a lifetime and I don't think I ever caught up with being left behind. So as I grew I filled the space this left me with kind dark eyes and noses as soft as velvet.

The legacy of health continued to haunt me and by the age of 12 there was heart infection, valve damage, major organ failure and childhood stroke. I survived and some, including even a doctor, said it was a miracle. But it did not feel like that to me as I found

myself alone in hospital for a second time with my life in the balance. But the horses in my head were there and they consoled me as I held on to them and the promise one day of one of my own.

Over the following years illness was never far enough away and never fully explained. But it didn't stop me from taking all the opportunities that came my way, although I think it made the taking of them more difficult. I married, had three children and raced with Nutty as an international endurance rider constantly pushing myself up and beyond our limits. Meanwhile, silently my body was bombarding itself with unsustainable and life threatening levels of cortisol, our naturally occurring stress hormone and it was all caused by a tiny undetected tumour beneath my brain. It is impossible to prove, but this tumour could have been with me from my earliest days. Eventually my mind and body would be at such a pitch that I would no longer sleep, my blood pressure would be off the scale and it would damage every system in my body.

Inexplicably I shared my tumour with my chestnut friend who had the same ticking away in her horse head. At the age of 23 she became suddenly lame and reluctant to move. The vet said she was just stiff but I disagreed, it was not like her. Next day she couldn't stand. I was sure this was laminitis but she wasn't the type, unless it was caused by cushings but she wasn't the type for that either. So I googled, discovered more, and concluded that it did look like cushings to me, and I noted that although incredibly rare people get it too.

The vet returned and although he agreed with my internet diagnosis it was too late for my lovely horse and I had to say goodbye to her that day. But I would remember the disease that took her from me and became convinced I might have it myself. My sympathetic doctor thought it unlikely but she referred me and after months of tests both in and out of hospital I was told it was true. As I was told I had cushings it was described to me as 'a devastating disease'.

And it is, thirty three days in hospital; removal of the wrong half of my pituitary gland, removal of both adrenal glands and eye surgery to repair the damage the tumour had done. Only this time the horses were far from me because there was no room in my cortisol filled mind.

I now have Addison's disease as a consequence of the adrenal removal. It is another life threatening condition given in exchange for my less desirable cushings. My adrenal glands went for stem cell research to help newborn babies and I have taken over from them, mimicking them as I give myself adjustable amounts of life essential cortisol until the day I die. Meanwhile I keep the tiny tumour beneath my brain, hopefully deactivated while I live in the hope that it never becomes active again.

When my illness was at its peak and I was raging with stress chemicals it was difficult to be with people or horses. I think the horses knew this and they withdrew from me. Happily after two years of recovery I am back with them and they are back with me. I have a new horse, a gift chosen by my husband and imported from Spain and she is exactly the horse I would have chosen for myself as a little girl. She is the Andalusian I would draw over and over again.

So that is my story, punctuated with horses and I keep the images in my mind which so often have been too difficult to understand or share. I think that is why I take pictures of other people and why now it is people and their horses. It is my way of exploring the relationships I have had in the past and understanding the ones I have today.

So I take my camera, I talk, I listen, I take some photographs and I look for the things I recognise in others and if it goes well I find a little bit more of myself. So when I say to you, "tell me about your horse" what I am really saying is "I want to know about what really matters to you and the things that you hold closest to your heart." In the answers there are stories like mine of childhood, family, failure, success, hope and recovery.

The Project

When I photograph people I want my pictures to be genuine, honest and as true a reflection of the person as possible. Interestingly, this can give the most flattering results. I like to clear away physical and mental clutter and just focus on the nature of whoever is on the other side of my lens. I often use a backdrop to minimise distraction or I choose to photograph people in a familiar place where they feel safe and relaxed. I talk to them and they talk to me, often forgetting the camera between us. Afterwards they say they are surprised to have enjoyed the experience and often say it hadn't felt like a photoshoot at all.

I wanted to use this same technique with horses and I wanted to take a different sort of horse portrait, one that might show us what was going on in the minds of these magnificent animals. So I started to approach people with my idea and rapidly it grew into a project taking me across Britain, to Ireland, the United States and North Africa.

I found myself a horse sized black muslin backdrop to cover walls and floors. I also made myself a mobile studio that I could take through an airport and onto a plane. Sometimes I thought I would use this, and at other times I would use the environment I was already immersed in.

The backdrop became increasingly significant as the project progressed. It defined a space and gave us all a zone to work in. Importantly, the horses had to trust us to walk onto it and the people were taken away from the familiar and had to trust me when I said it was a good idea. Some horses and some people took a little more persuading but I had no refusals and we all got there in the end.

I've spent my life watching the faces of horses and people and I think horses have a range of facial expression most people fail to notice. We are all in tune with the ears of a horse and we humans use them as a safety mechanism. We look at them to tell us what our horses are thinking and feeling. Ears forward means engaged and interested. Ears up means possibly dozy and maybe relaxed. Ears back means I want to kick or bite you.

But watch horses together and you will see them communicate with each other using the entirety of their face including the teeth, nose, mouth and tongue. There is tension and relaxation in the jaw and above the eyes. We mask that with bits, bridles and nosebands and in a picture the loss is ours. As the project progressed, I wanted to remove the tack and photograph the horses with total freedom of expression. When you take the accessories off a horse, it goes off duty and you can see what it really thinks. A horse will run from things it is afraid of but if a horse likes you it will stay with you.

Towards the end of the project I went to North Africa where I was invited to photograph some of the most extraordinarily beautiful horses. Sadly, there is no place for them in this work because they were fearful of their handlers.

This book and the pictures it contains are simply about all that is good between us and horses in our lives.

Louis Muspratt and Dance Floor King

For my first shoot I went to see Nick Mitchell, a second generation racing trainer who lives close to my Dorset home. Our daughters are friends and we admit to each other that we both had pictures of Red Rum on our bedroom walls as children. I have photographed Nick before and I like the way he is with his horses.

I explained my ideas and Nick was willing to see what we could achieve. He cleared a barn and introduced me to jockey Louis Muspratt and the horse Dance Floor King.

Louis has ridden as both amateur and professional whilst suffering multiple injuries as a consequence but he says he has to keep riding because there is just simply nothing better.

The shoot was a success with Dance Floor King happily following Nick onto the muslin to be photographed with Louis. Horse racing is not a sport known for tenderness between horse and rider but I had found genuine affection here.

Sorrel Russell, Hotwash and Serge

With Sorrel I found such freedom, connection and simplicity. She is in tune with her horses and they are with her. I photographed Sorrel with Serge, her unusual thoroughbred gypsy cob cross. Serge has a blue or 'wall' eye, which has traditionally been thought of as a weakness and viewed with suspicion, but Sorrel thinks he is beautiful, and he is.

I had not anticipated photographing Sorrel with Hotwash, the family pony, but he proved to be increasingly irresistible as he made his presence known.

Once we decided to include him he was happy to join Sorrel on the sofa stored in his barn.

Claire Brougham

Claire is a top British Polo player. She's based in Surrey and takes her ponies as far away as Spain and rides others as far away as China. I met her and her ponies on a hot bright day at her yard.

Bright sun is usually the photographer's enemy but it somehow encouraged the togetherness of this shoot as the horses stood together in each other's shade. We talk about a string of polo ponies and I could see the way Claire's horses behaved as a group, moving around her with confidence but following her lead. It was as if these horses were connected to each other and to her.

Henriette Von Stockhausen, Rosamund Collins and Saville Row

Henriette Von Stockhausen is one of few civilians to have exercised horses for the British Army. For 12 years she rode out every morning in Hyde Park for the Household Cavalry while most of London still slept. She also rode for the Light Cavalry in Windsor Park and this brought her into contact with Rosamund Collins, a dressage trainer and teacher of sidesaddle. Friendship grew and sidesaddle demonstrations at Windsor before the Queen followed.

I met them both in Windsor with Saville Row, a stunning horse trained in dressage and sidesaddle by Rosamund for his owner. Saville Row, known as Rupert, was beautifully presented. I could see that there must have been many hours of preparation before I arrived. So it was no surprise when Rosamund explained that the connection she has with her horses begins with the day-to-day care she gives them.

Rupert loved the attention, and seemed to know exactly what was expected of him.

Henriette Von Stockhausen and Saville Row

Rosamund Collins and Saville Row

The Urban Cowboy

I had heard about the urban cowboys of Dublin. They were described to me as the descendants of settled travellers who live on housing estates on the outskirts of the city.

They are young, male and have horses in their blood. Although they may seem to have few opportunities, they have their horses and they take huge pride in them. I found a charity willing to help me find some of these boys and they explained to me how these horses are frequently impounded and taken away from the boys and off the streets.

Certainly some of these horses would have better lives away from the waste ground of a housing estate but there was something very good that I could see happening here too. I was told that these ponies, bought for just a few euros, were often all that these boys had. I was left to wonder if more could be done to use the good that I could see and keep the horses with the boys and enhance both of their lives.

One of the boys was riding his horse on a grass verge while his friends played football and he was happy to be photographed in this public place. But he refused to tell me his name or that of his horse, perhaps for fear that his horse would be taken from him.

Ed, Luli and Anouska Loveridge, Chester and Partytime

Jemma Loveridge has three children, ponies and a horse of her own. She has a home which is overflowing with cups, ribbons and horse enthusiasm. Jemma also makes the most beautiful hats from a workshop close to her stables, and at the time we met she had been making hats for Ascot.

Chester is Jemma's horse and big enough for all three children. He was completely calm and ideal for the photoshoot as he showed the utmost patience and kindness towards all three children.

Partytime is a jumping pony standing at just 12.2 and her enormous jump has taken her young rider to Hickstead, the Horse of The Year Show and Olympia. She has had other homes before this one and soon the Loveridge children will be too big for her and she will move on. So this was an interesting meeting between Luli, Partytime and an old rocking horse we found at the back of the barn who looked like she had been loved by many children too.

Ed, Luli and Anouska Loveridge and Chester

Luli Loveridge and Partytime

Lily Gibbens and Otis

Lily and Otis are both six years old. Otis belongs to Lliy's mother and he stands at a magnificent 17.2. He is so gentle with Lily and I wonder if this is because he knows his size and his strength is so much greater than hers. It is easy to see how safe she feels with him. There can be few creatures so large we can trust like this with someone so small.

Warren Scofield, Iggy Madden and Cairdiuil

Warren is a vet based in Kildare, Ireland and Cairdiuil is his racehorse, trained by Iggy Madden. All three joined me for the shoot at Warren's equine hospital. I had just been to see Cairdiuil up on the Curragh beforehand, where he'd galloped a mile but he had plenty of energy left for the photoshoot.

Cairdiuil is small for a thoroughbred but big when it comes to personality, and he is owned by Warren and three of his longstanding friends. Cairdiuil had a mixed start in life, with a maiden win followed by some disappointing performances. Fortunately one of Warren's specialisms is bone scanning, which can be used as a preventative diagnostic tool for sportshorses.

So when the horse came to them as a three-year-old Warren bone-scanned and, with Iggy, built a program that would meet the needs of Cairdiuil's body and mind. This included specific training plus regular time at grass in the company of other horses.

Once happy Cairdiuil began to perform and he has since gone on to be a success with four wins to date.

He's still running at ten years old and enjoys plenty of regular time off in the field with his friends.

It was lovely to see Iggy and Cairdiuil together, both of whom were free of all tack. These two know each other very well but, at the same time, it was as if they were meeting each other for the first time.

The attachment between Warren and his horse is obvious and I was not surprised in the least when Warren explained to me he would still have a home for Cairdiuil once his racing days were over.

Iggy Maddon and Cairdiuill

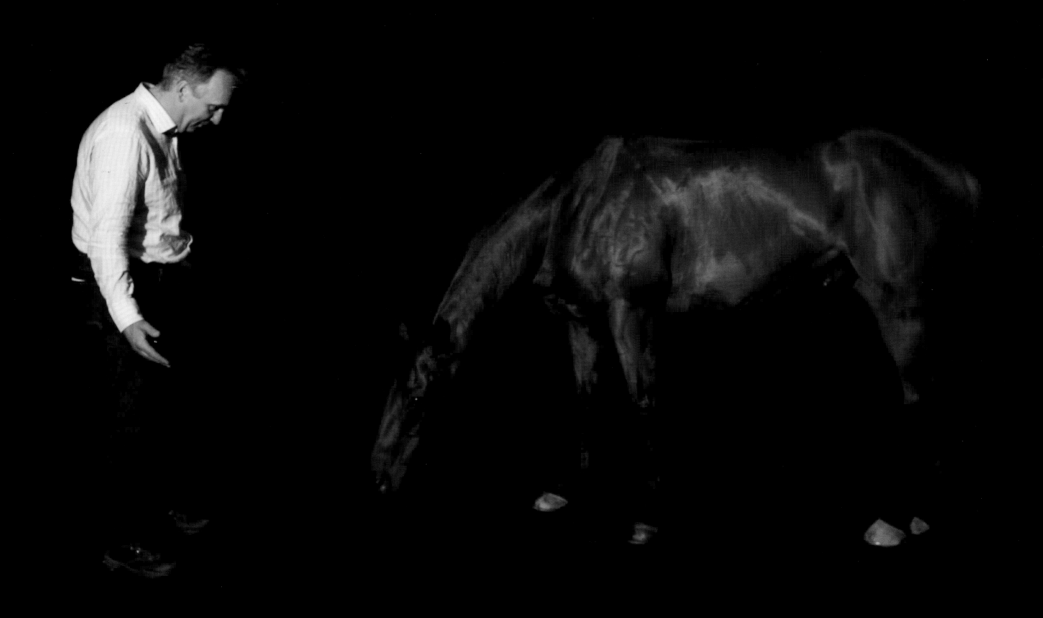

Warren Scofield and Cairdiuill

Richard Eames and Elizabeth

There is something very special about Richard and Elizabeth. Richard has a career with horses which began in the Household Cavalry and which brings him today to an English woodland where he works alongside Elizabeth as a horse logger, extracting timber in the same way it has been done for centuries.

Elizabeth is a gypsy cob and together, with Richard, they make a true working pair. They work together in places inaccessible to machinery on sensitive, steep or difficult sites.

I spent the day with Richard and Elizabeth in a Shropshire woodland, where I witnessed the elegance about the pair of them; with the slightest command Elizabeth moves her enormous feathered legs laterally with the precision of a dressage horse. As she moved, Richard stepped sideways with her in his heavy boots as he navigated his way through the wood just behind her.

Amy Panter, Jack, Isis and Malaguena

There is so much beauty in the human and horse forms and I wanted to find a way to make that combined beauty work together. Amy is a talented aerial acrobat and an equestrian performer and she was willing to come and explore this unity in a shoot with my horses at my home.

Jack is my daughter's Welsh pony. I bought him as an unhanded yearling at a pony sale and he has proved himself to be the safest pony for the smallest child. Isis is our Anglo Arab, named after the Egyptian goddess and ridden by my husband. Malaguenua is mine. She was born in Spain and destined for the bullring and I can see from the scars on her face that her start with people was not a good one, but she knows now that we mean her no harm.

I have a sand turnout and riding area in the middle of which stands a horse chestnut tree. Beneath the tree is the place where the horses gather to stand together and shelter from sun and rain. I made a stage under the canopy of the tree for Amy so that she could work from the floor and the branches. I let the horses free to see what they would make of this extraordinary creature hanging from their tree. There was very little direction in this shoot; it was lovely to see the natural beauty and expression between Amy and the horses.

Heather Jansch

Not everyone I photographed was with a real horse. I have been impressed by Heather Jansch and her work after seeing a horse she had created at the Eden project in Cornwall. I wanted to include her in this book because her horses are as real to me as any I have ever met. In her sculptures I can see the connection I have been trying to find in my pictures of real horses and people.

I visited her at her home in a Devon valley where she works surrounded by her horses and the garden she has created.

What was initially meant to be a few hours turned into a day spent together as we began to talk about our horses and our lives. She introduced me to her horses sculpted out of driftwood and weathered timber and as we worked our way through her wooden herd Heather told me the story of each horse in turn while I tried to decide who was best to photograph with Heather. We came to Beltaine Juno, a hunter mare who stood benevolently above both of us. It could only be her I decided, and Heather said she thought she would be the one I would choose.

Belatane Juno was one of her earliest horses and Heather had made her, sold her and exported her to America years before. Only Heather had missed her and wanted her back and she told me the story about how she had eventually been able to bring her home where she belongs.

Edward Cazalet

Horses are engrained in the life of Sir Edward, a retired High Court Judge who spent his formative years growing up in the Queen Mother's training yard.

His father, Peter, was her trainer, training in all more than two hundred and fifty winners for her. She was a regular visitor to the childhood home to see the likes of Devon Loch. Devon Loch, who is remembered by the nation as the horse who fell dramatically short of Grand National victory, is also remembered by Edward as an individual and impressive horse.

As a young boy aged eight he had a serious hip complaint. The treatment was a year's immobilisation in bed but he spent that time reading all he could, learning about horses.

He also had the good fortune to possess a 14.2 mare, which Elizabeth Taylor would borrow when she came to stay for weekends.

Before becoming a barrister, Edward was a highly successful amateur steeplechase jockey, riding many winners and ultimately having to ride at level weights against the professionals. He holds the record of having been the only High Court judge to have ridden at the annual Cheltenham Festival meeting. On retirement, amongst further appointments, he became chairman of the Jockey Club Appeal Board and The Injured Jockeys fund.

The Cazalets have no real horses now, but when I visited for lunch I saw many others and these hang on the walls or stand outside. So it was with these horses the pictures were taken.

Troytown GreyAbbey Hospital & The Kildare Blood Donors

I was fortunate enough to spend time with vet Warren Scofield at the Troytown GreyAbbey Hospital. He was accompanied by his partners, staff and horses in a centre where clients included studs, racehorse trainers, sports horse breeders and eventers. Interestingly, Warren only unearthed his empathy with horses once he had trained as a vet. Now, they fill his life. He works with horses, he owns his own racehorse, and has a young family who ride.

At the hospital there are three very special horses who help the vets in their work, Little John, Reno Tinto and Cato. The blood donors have reached a certain level of celebrity, as the only horses to do this work full time, occasionally giving a little of their blood to save some of the finest horses in Ireland.

They came individually to the hospital to be euthanised, but at the request of the hospital team, and with the owners' consent, they now live a contented, useful life together.

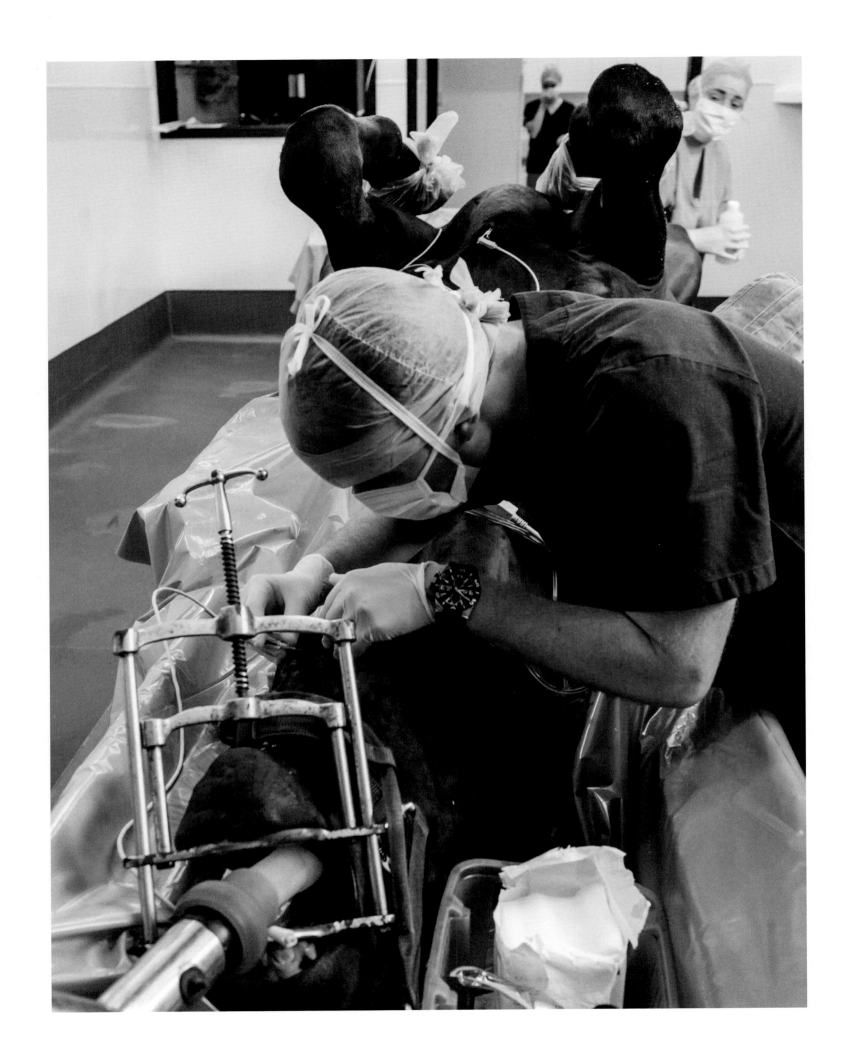

Kelly Marks and American Pie

Kelly pioneers 'Intelligent Horsemanship' and is inspired by horse behaviour and psychology. She teaches and demonstrates, putting together courses, writing books, holding clinics and working to improve the relationship people have with their horses.

Kelly has a long history with horses and was a successful show jumper in her early life before becoming a winning jockey. She gave up riding with a whip in 1991, deciding it was simply wrong, and went on to some of her biggest racing successes without it. Pie is her horse and despite a lifetime with horses he is the only horse she has ever been able to call her own. She describes Pie as the childhood dream she never grew out of and I know exactly what she means.

Kelly and Pie were the perfect combination for me and by using a round pen, Pie was free to approach Kelly and be with her as he chose. He wanted to be with her and the affection they have for each other is obvious.

Richard Waygood and Prospector Joe

Richard is impressive and he is a truly international equestrian who has had a career spent discovering new possibilities with horses. He joined the army at 16 and worked his way to become the Riding Master of the Household Cavalry Mounted Regiment, choreographing the musical ride and even putting a performance on ice at St Moritz. He added an electric guitarist to the traditional proceedings of the musical ride and taught his favourite horse to jump a single sword in the ground. He has competed at Badminton Horse Trials as a serving army officer and has been awarded an MBE for his services to equestrianism. Today he is a trainer and is the Team Manager and chef d'Equipe for the British Olympic dressage team.

I visited him at his gleaming training yard while preparations for Rio Olympics were underway. This was the only yard I visited with polished champagne glasses by the tack room sink and I hoped these were a good omen. I photographed him with Prospector Joe.

Will Bryer and George

Will Bryer is Master and Huntsman of the Cattistock Hunt. I had an out of season shoot with him and his horse George at the hunt kennels. It was in the summer so there was no hunting and I was able to meet Will and George off-duty, removed from the costume and tradition that is associated with hunting.

What I uncovered was a genuine pair; a man who was casually dressed and George the horse wearing only his summer coat. This was the most companionable pair I photographed for this book and George was perfectly contented to stand by Will for as long as it took.

I have always thought that we give horses names for our own benefit and that they never seem to understand them or respond to them. But I wondered with George whether he knew his name because Will spoke it to him, so incredibly quietly and gently over and over again and it held his attention. Perhaps all horses would like to be spoken to as softly as Will speaks to George.

William Fox-Pitt and Chilli Morning

By this stage, I was realising that it was the horses who were leading the shoots. This was no more so than with Chilli Morning, who I photographed before they left for Rio to represent Great Britain in the Olympics.

I was honoured that they had given me the time for a shoot. These were busy days in the Fox-Pitt yard but they had made space for me that day even though there was anticipation of departure in the air. It was difficult to believe that less than a year earlier William had been in a coma in hospital having suffered a head injury following a fall.

Chilli was spoken of by all as an absolute gentleman who knows his job and simply does it very well. Unusually for an eventer, he is a stallion who events but also performs stud duties for part of the year.

I have always thought that stallions communicate more with their mouths than other horses and Chilli, although co-operative, was a little bored by the photographic process. So, after giving us a little of his time, he ended the shoot himself by lowering his head and, with his teeth, ripping a large hole in the backdrop.

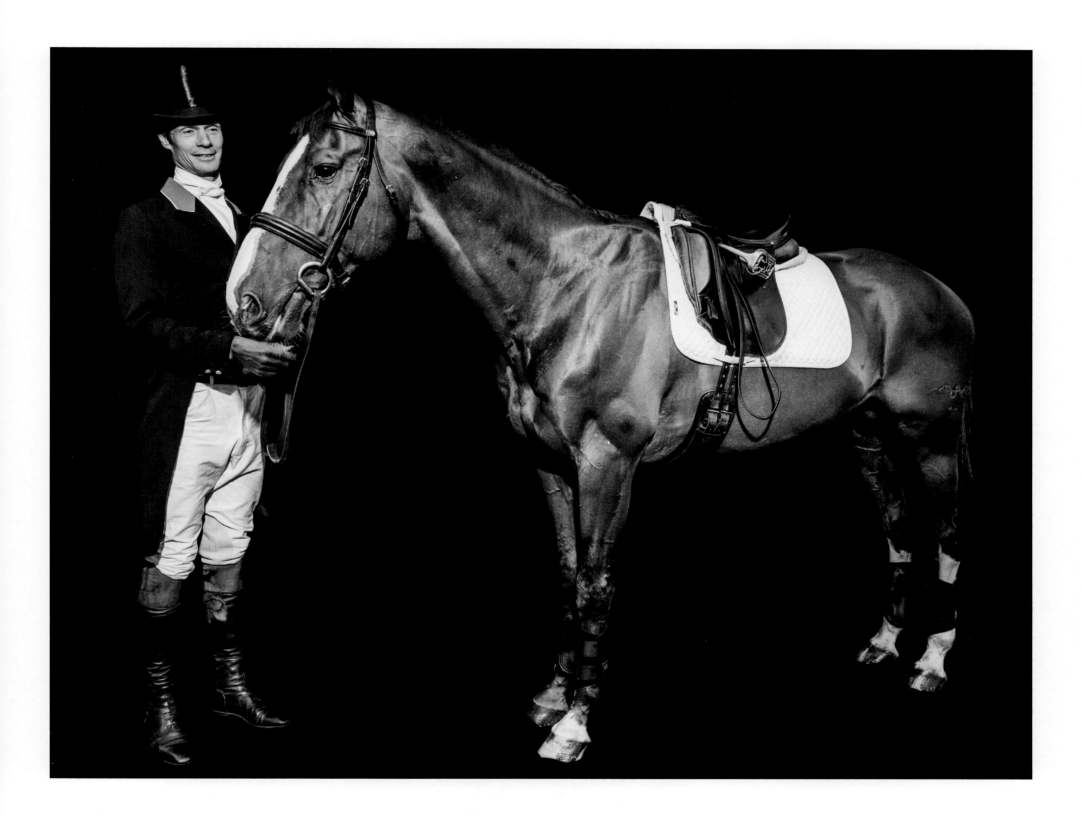

Monty Roberts and Shy Boy

Kelly Marks put me in touch with Monty and he immediately invited me to spend time with him at his Ranch, Flag is Up Farms, in Solvang, California. I spent four days close to him, watching him and taking part in the work he does. It was a generous offering from the man known as the world's greatest horse whisperer of both his time and of himself.

In California I saw untouched mustangs 'gentled' as they accepted their first human contact. There were horses who willingly met their first rider and horses damaged by people who had regained their trust in front of my eyes. I went into the round pen with horses and I met Monty's family, his students and the war veterans he works with. I could see that people and horses find themselves at Flag Is Up Farms for a myriad of reasons but once there they can each discover something unique in the connection they find.

He says his ideas are simple and that they are based on his understanding of equine communication. His message is of non-violence for both horses and humans. He has spent a lifetime observing horse communication and has learnt to respond to horses in ways that they understand. As he does he enters their world and, once joined, he builds relationships based on willingness and co-operation. Monty Roberts is called a horse whisperer but, more than that, he's a listener, listening to people as well as horses.

Monty achieved international recognition after he was invited to demonstrate his methods to Her Majesty, the Queen at Windsor Castle. Today, at the age of 81, he continues to spread his message across the world. In the last 27 years he has demonstrated his methods in 41 countries, in front of 3.6 million people and worked with thousands of horses.

Shy Boy is the Nevada mustang who starred in a BBC documentary experiment which was set up to see if Monty could successfully join up with a wild horse without using force or enclosure. Within three days Shy Boy had accepted Monty as his companion and rider and today he continues to live with Monty at Flag is Up Farm, enjoying his celebrity status.

As we prepared for the shoot, I put up the backdrop and Monty let Shy Boy loose. Shy Boy got to the backdrop first, needing no encouragement, and he inspected it thoroughly before Monty joined him. He has total confidence in Monty; the bond between the two is so visible. Once we thought we had finished the shoot, Monty and I began to talk but Shy Boy seemed to just want Monty to himself and simply would not leave him alone, so we carried on taking pictures. I think that some of the best pictures were taken then.

Later it seemed only natural to me that Shy Boy would join Monty at the bar. Monty agreed to take him into the saloon, which is part of his house, on our final evening for an extra picture. It turned into a bit of an occasion and we were joined by Monty's family, colleagues and students. Least surprised was Shy Boy, who was so totally at ease stepping alongside Monty into his human world.

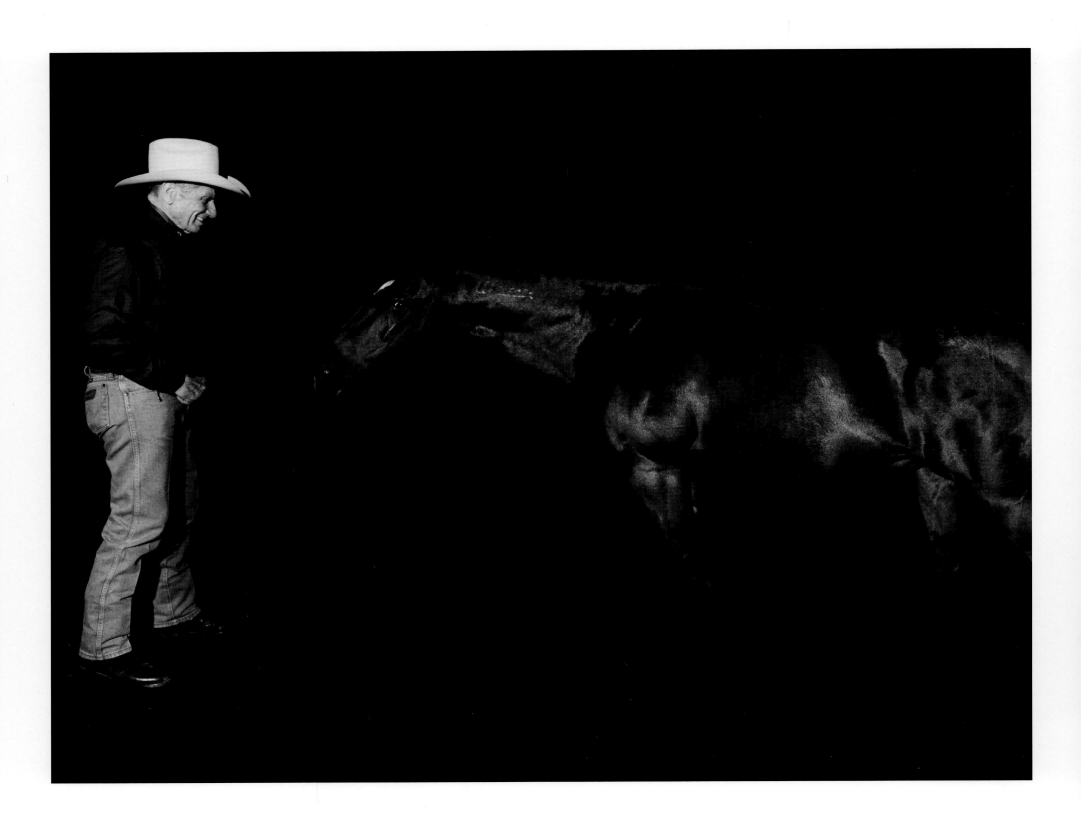

Epilogue

I ask the people I photograph: why horses? I only wish I could ask the horses too.

I think the real answer remains a mystery, stretching back thousands of years to the time when one of us first thought to tame a horse and climb onto its back. The men I ask speak of possibilities, speed and partnership while the women speak of touch, power and togetherness. They all know the unspoken understanding. There are many who will not understand this book or know what it means to be at one with one of these magical creatures or to have felt a horse turn towards them. If you have shared this book with me and felt those things, I thank you. We have experienced something ancient and beautiful and I believe that we are the most fortunate of people.

Afterword

I've been working alongside and riding horses my whole career. Whether they are Household Cavalry horses being trained for ceremonial duties, thoroughbred eventers learning to push themselves above, beyond and over obstacles the like of which often made my eyes water let alone theirs, or Grand Prix dressage horses balancing on the tip of control and equine possibility; all have been both unique and wonderfully, majestically, united by the same sense of power, elegance and character.

It has been a privilege to devote my working life to the horse, and it is a privilege to experience Lucy's powerful and sensitive interpretation of the animal I know so well.

It's rare to find a photographer who captures their essence quite so successfully as Lucy Sewill. Her passion and background with horses have given her a clear advantage when it comes to capturing our equestrian friends.

Richard Waygood MBE